crafty girl™

slumber parties

crafty girl™

slumber parties

things to make and do

by Jennifer Traig

CHRONICLE BOOKS
SAN FRANCISCO

Library of Congress Cataloging-in-Publication Data available.

ISBN 0-8118-3571-5

Manufactured in China

Line drawings by Stephanie Sadler
Designed and illustrated by Gayle Steinbeigle, Protopod Design

Distributed in Canada by Raincoast Books
9050 Shaughnessy Street
Vancouver, British Columbia V6P 6E5

10 9 8 7 6 5 4 3 2 1

Chronicle Books LLC
85 Second Street
San Francisco, California 94105
www.chroniclebooks.com

acknowledgments

Thanks to the party people: Alain Traig, Judy Traig, Victoria Traig, Peter McGrath, Wendy McGrath, Dan McGrath, Maureen Neff, Tim Neff, Courtney Vaughn, and Mark Bellias. Corner slices of cake with extra frosting roses go to Jodi Davis, Mikyla Bruder, Gayle Steinbeigle, and Stephanie Sadler.

table of contents

*A*s pillow fighting your favorite sport? Can you make a meal out of pretzels and Pixy Stix? Are you surgically attached to your sleeping bag? No doubt about it: You're a slumber party animal. You're a connoisseur, and you know that potato chips, pizza, and prank calls may make a perfectly pleasant Saturday night, but they do not make a slumber party. A slumber party is much more special than that. That's where *Crafty Girl: Slumber Parties* comes in, with plenty of ideas to make your slumber parties sparkle. Consider this your invitation to nights you'll never forget.

Maybe you're a hostess with the mostest, or maybe you're a hostess with not so much. Whatever your entertaining style, *Crafty Girl: Slumber Parties* has lots of suggestions for you. If your idea of party dress is an oversized T-shirt and boxer shorts, consider a casual party theme like Starry Starry Night (page 112), a backyard camp-out. You probably have all the supplies you need on hand right now. If you're really spontaneous, call your friends this minute and make it a come-as-you-are event. Or perhaps you prefer a party that's a bit more posh. A Formal Film Festival (page 61) or a Midnight Tea Party (page 46) should be just your cup of fun. Get all gussied up and enjoy fancy-pants finger foods. Slumber parties can be ever so civilized. Or not. Either way, don't think of these party plans as strict agendas. Make them your own. It's your party, and you get to call the shots.

Let's begin with the most important subject: the chow. Sure, your friends love you, but we all know the real reason they're coming to your slumber party is to eat your food. Forget a sensible dinner; slumber parties are all about the snack attack. Deliver with lots of crunchy munchies. If you feel the need for a vitamin or two, try veggies and dip. Otherwise, stick to the two basic food groups: deep-fried and chocolate-covered. If your friends are a picky bunch, make-your-own-dinner bars are a great way to get everyone fed fast. Put out all the fixin's for sandwiches, burritos, baked potatoes, or sundaes and let everyone make their own meal. If you want the meal to be the main event, consider a food-themed party like Sweet Dreams (page 14) or Kitchen Olympics (page 31). Your guests will make the meal in a cutthroat cooking competition. And if it's not edible, you can always order a pizza.

Go ahead and chow down—you'll need to keep your strength up. Slumber parties are the entertaining equivalent of a marathon. You've got a minimum of twelve hours to fill, and you can be sure almost none of that will be spent sleeping. Most of it will be spent in front of the TV. What did people do at slumber parties before the VCR was invented? Maybe they painted cave walls or hunted woolly mammoths; we don't know. We're just thankful we live in an age where *Bring It On* is available on DVD. Take advantage of technology and rent a stack of movies. Get a mix of new releases and old favorites. You can't see *Sixteen Candles* too many times.

Or maybe you can. When your brain starts to feel as fried as your party snacks, it's time for something a little more active. *Crafty Girl: Slumber Parties* has tons of ideas for high-stakes slumber party games. Play variations on old standbys, like Food Truth or Dare (page 33) or Audio Scavenger Hunt (page 119). Or play something new and exciting, like Kitchen Commando (page 34). Here's a Crafty Girl Party Tip: Games are always more fun when they end with prizes, so stock up on little gifts to give the winners (and the losers, too. *Everybody* likes free stuff!).

What's better than a slumber party favor? A slumber party favor you make yourself. Crafting is a great slumber party activity. It gives you something to do between meals and keeps your hands busy while you watch movies.

Host a Fashion Fantasia (page 39) and craft your own high-style Jean Genie designer wear (page 43). Host a Bliss-Out Spa Party (page 89) and craft your own Overnight Repair Kit beauty treatments (page 95). And if you're *really* crafty, host a craft-themed party like a Beadapalooza (page 53), an all-night crafty free-for-all. It's a Crafty Girl's dream come true.

So let's get this party started! You may have all the supplies in the house already. If you don't, a party-supply store is a good place to start. You can stock up on streamers and balloons and a ton of things you didn't even know you needed, like grass skirts, googly-eyed glasses, and plastic cowboy hats. Once you've got your decorations and party favors, head to the craft store for supplies like rhinestones for the Rhinestone Rocker Tee (page 86) or fabric for Castaway Clothes (page 117). If you're on a budget (or if you just have a taste for the retro stuff), comb thrift stores and garage sales for cheap and funky decorations and crafting supplies. Finally, you'll want to hit the supermarket. Spend a lot of time in the snack aisle. Remember: Fried foods and fun-size candy bars are the glue that holds all slumber parties together, so stock up.

Finally, a word of caution. Some of the projects in this book require a stove; others require pointy things like pins and scissors. Be careful handling anything that could hurt you, and make sure there's an adult around to supervise the proceedings. Stitches and first-degree burns make lousy slumber party souvenirs, so play safe.

Party on!

Sweet Dreams

Who can take an ordinary evening and turn it into the best slumber party of all time? The Candy Man can.

Welcome to your ultimate fantasy: a candy-themed slumber party. That's right—it's twelve hours of nonstop sugar. Start with an all-candy dinner. Then play candy games, make candy crafts, watch candy-themed movies, and rock out to candy-themed tunes. The next day you'll feel terrible and your teeth will be wearing tiny fuzzy sweaters, but who cares? It's candy!

Menu

Chocolate Soup*

Candy pizza
(make a crust from a brownie mix or cookie dough, spread on some frosting, then top with your favorite candies; you could even cut little "pepperoni" circles from Fruit Roll-Ups)

Candy salad
(toss together a gorp-style mixture of chocolate chips, malted milk balls, and M&M's)

*Recipe follows

Invitation

Slide the wrapper off a plain chocolate bar and tape your handmade invitation in its place. Make it look as much like the original wrapper as possible but with your own twist: "Ingredients: 7 crazy girls, 1 crazy night, and 50 pounds of sugar."

This party is easy as pie to plan. All you need is a sweet tooth and a shopping cart full of treacly treats. Your guests will probably be too spun on sugar to notice what your house looks like, but if you feel the need to decorate, a piñata and a few bouquets of Pixy Stix should suffice. If you're really ambitious, buy a few M&M-patterned sleeping bags. But who are we kidding? Everyone will be way too wired to sleep. Sweet!

Music

The Archies, "Sugar, Sugar" and, of course, Bow Wow Wow, "I Want Candy"

Games

Candy isn't just a snack; it's also a sport. Spice up your slumber party with some competitive candy action. You could play a real-life version of Candyland, making the board out of graham crackers and using chocolate kisses and hard candies as playing pieces. Or play Candy Concentration and hide pairs of fun-size candy bars under little cups; find a match and you get to eat them. If you're looking for something a little more extreme, turn up the heat. Microwave Jolly Rancher sticks until soft, then twist them into shapes (but be careful not to burn yourself). Or play Peeps Jousting: Jab a toothpick each into two Peeps, and then place them face to face in the microwave, with the toothpicks touching as though the Peeps were fencing. Turn the microwave on for a minute or so and watch them go at it. Trust us: It's better than TV.

chocolate
Soup

Chocolate soup may sound weird, but it's actually a very old recipe. Thicker than hot chocolate, thinner than pudding, it's like a bowl of dream-come-true. Vive le chocolat!

You will need:

1 tablespoon cornstarch

2¼ cups half-and-half, plus more to taste

1 pound unsweetened chocolate, chopped

2½ cups sugar, plus more to taste

2 teaspoons vanilla extract

12 shortbread cookies, broken into pieces

[1] Dissolve the cornstarch in ¼ cup of the half-and-half and set aside.

[2] In a saucepan, combine the chocolate, sugar, and the 2 cups of half-and-half over low heat, stirring until the mixture is melted and well blended. Mix in the vanilla, then add the cornstarch mixture. Continue to cook over low heat, stirring constantly, until the soup is the consistency of heavy cream. Taste and add more sugar or cream if needed.

[3] Spoon the soup into bowls and top with shortbread "croutons." Then serve. Soup's on!

Serves 8.

the art of
candy

Music is nice, ballet is lovely, and painting is fine, but as far as we're concerned the only true art is candy. Now you can make it into sculpture. Whip up a batch of modeling fondant, a sugary dough that's easy to mold into almost any shape. Modeling fondant is marzipan's country cousin. While marzipan (almond paste) is great for sculpting, modeling fondant is better because you probably already have all the ingredients on hand—and it tastes like frosting. The only drawback is that it can get pretty soft. Just keep it cold and you'll have no problem.

You will need:

⅓ cup margarine or butter, at room temperature

⅓ cup light corn syrup

Pinch of salt

½ teaspoon vanilla extract

3½ cups powdered sugar, plus more as needed

Food coloring

[1] Combine the margarine, corn syrup, salt,
vanilla, and powdered sugar. Mix well. If the
dough is too soft, add more powdered sugar. It
should be about the consistency of play dough.

[2] Divide the dough and add food coloring to
make various colors. Then chill, chill, chill.
The colder it is, the easier it is to work with.

[3] Dust your hands with powdered sugar and
sculpt the dough into shapes, such as minia-
ture apples, oranges, and bananas; a bust of
yourself; a reproduction of Michelangelo's
David; or whatever you like.

[4] Refrigerate the shapes until you're
ready to eat them.

Serves 8.

bon bon
baubles

Candy is a fabulous material to fashion into jewelry. It's pretty, it smells wonderful, and if you are ever in a hypoglycemic pinch, you can eat your earrings. Candy can be made into all sorts of lovely ornaments. Try gluing M&M's or Skittles onto barrettes. (But be sure to shellac them, and don't wear them on hot days. Melty chocolate in your hair—yuck.) You could string any candy with a hole in the center onto elastic cord to make necklaces or bracelets. Or make these funky and flavorful earrings.

You will need:

Straight pin

2 wrapped candies for each guest
(use candies like Tootsie Rolls,
Starlight Mints, or sour balls)

2 jump rings for each guest

Round-nose pliers (optional)

2 earring findings for each guest

[1] Using the straight pin, make a tiny hole in a candy wrapper, about ⅛ inch down from one edge.

[2] Pry a jump ring open with your fingers or the pliers, if using, and thread it through the hole you just made. Thread an earring finding onto the jump ring. Then use your fingers or the pliers to firmly pinch the jump ring closed.

[3] Repeat with the other piece of candy and earring finding.

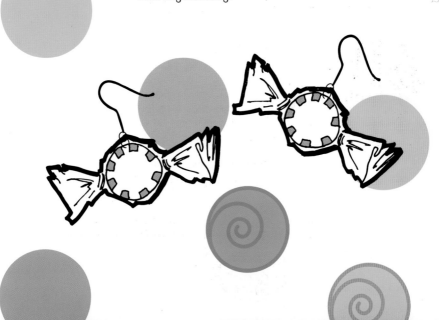

Arabian Nights

Are you up for a
magic carpet ride?
Then this party
is for you.

This party is a tribute to Scheherazade, an ancient, fictional character who practically invented the bedtime story and introduced the world to girl power at the same time. Beautiful and brilliant, she was devastated when the sultan of her homeland began killing his brides the morning after he wed them. She bravely asked to be his next wife. On their wedding night, she began telling a story. It was so good he spared her life until the next night. She continued the story, and again he spared her. On and on the story went, for 1,001 nights, and the killing stopped.

Movies

Aladdin

Lawrence of Arabia

Menu

Hummus and baba ganoush
(from the deli section of the supermarket)

Tabbouleh *(from a mix)*

Warm pita bread

Arabian Bites*

Baklava *(store-bought)*

Pomegranate punch
(mix grenadine with lemon-lime soda)

Chai tea

*Recipe follows

We celebrate Scheherazade with this extra-special party. Unless you have a genie, it will take a bit of work on your part, but the payoff is a party that will rock the Casbah. Do your hair in an I-Dream-of-Jeannie ponytail, and don your best harem pants. Decorate the house to resemble the inside of a genie's bottle. Tack bedsheets

Invitation

Why send your invitation in an ordinary envelope when you can put it in a genie's bottle instead? Cover small glass or plastic bottles with gold paint and flat-back gems. Write up the invitations in Arabic-looking script on parchment paper. Roll the invitations up and insert one in each bottle, leaving the end sticking out so the lucky recipient will be able to retrieve it.

to the ceiling and walls to create an impromptu Bedouin tent. Keep the lighting low, and drape scarves around the room. Arrange pretty pillows in a circle. Serve dinner on a low table, and sit on the floor. Play Middle Eastern music and practice your belly-dancing moves. If you are going all out, hire a dancer to give your guests a lesson. If not, rent a videotape. Craft a Belly Chain (page 29) and try some Persian Princess Body Art (page 27) to give your dance a little extra sparkle.

A perfect Persian party? Your wish is our command.

Music

Christina Aguilera, "Genie in a Bottle"

The Clash, "Rock the Casbah"

Or pick up some Middle Eastern compilations from the world music section

Games

When the party starts winding down, crank things up with a round of Scheherazade, a zany storytelling game. The first player begins by making up a story. The person sitting next to her continues the story, and so on and so on. Make the story as outrageous as possible, including all your friends as characters. Send them to Mars or Morocco, and make sure they're accompanied by their favorite celebrities.

arabian
bites

These little morsels are Middle Eastern magic. A rich, delicious cheese mixture is sandwiched between layers of phyllo dough and butter and baked until melty. If we had three wishes, this is what we'd wish for all three times.

You will need:

2 cups crumbled feta cheese

2 cups cottage cheese

5 eggs, lightly beaten

1 cup butter

1 pound phyllo dough, thawed to room temperature

[1] Preheat the oven to 375° F.

[2] In a mixing bowl, combine the feta cheese, cottage cheese, and eggs. Mix well and set aside.

continued on next page

[3] Melt the butter. Brush the bottom and sides of a 9-by-13-inch pan generously with butter. Lay a sheet of phyllo in the pan. It will be bigger than the pan, so let the edges of the dough climb the sides of the pan. Brush the phyllo generously with butter. Place another sheet of phyllo on top and brush with more butter. Repeat until you have 8 sheets stacked in the pan. Spread half the cheese mixture over the phyllo.

[4] Place another 8 sheets of buttered phyllo on top, then spread the rest of the cheese mixture over the top. Continue to top with buttered sheets of phyllo until the pan is full. Be sure to butter the top sheet. Pinch the side edges of the phyllo down. Bake for 45 minutes.

[5] Cut into diamonds, triangles, or squares, and serve hot.

Serves 8.

persian princess
body art

We just love henna body painting, but let's face it: mehndi is messy. It's hard to make those delicate designs when you're working with great globs of henna paste, and it's easy to get the dye all over the white couch while you're waiting for it to dry. So we came up with a very untraditional alternative we call the Henna Penna method. Simply draw your mehndi design on your skin, using an ordinary nontoxic marker. It's cheating, sure, but it gets the job done, and nobody will know the difference. Use brown or black for an authentic henna look. Or, if you're feeling more punk than Persian, use bright crazy colors like hot pink or turquoise. Then glue on some sparkly body jewels. I Dream of Jeannie's got nothing on you, glitter girl.

You will need:

Nontoxic, nonpermanent markers with a fairly fine tip

Flat-back rhinestones

Eyelash glue

continued on next page

[1] First, make sure your skin is clean and dry. Then get your marker and make mehndi magic. Draw pretty designs on your hands, arms, feet, or, if you're planning on doing a belly dance later, around your navel. If you're not ambidextrous or especially limber, you might need a friend to help with your hands and midriff.

[2] Ornament your designs by gluing flat-back rhinestones to your skin using eyelash glue. You could even glue a few stones on your face. Just be careful not to get the glue in your eyes.

[3] That's it! When you get tired of being a walking work of art, peel off the jewels and wash the ink off with soap and water. Be warned: The ink might stick around for a day or two, so this is a bad project to do, say, the night before your cousin's wedding, unless your family is cool with kooky body art.

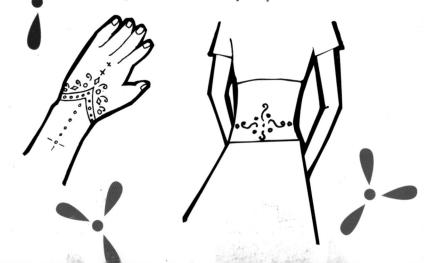

belly chain

Your neck, wrists, and ankles get to wear pretty chains; why shouldn't your waist wear one, too? Craft this beautiful beaded chain to make your belly dance really sparkle. Pair it with harem pants or a low-waisted gauzy skirt and you'll look Persia-perfect.

You will need:

Measuring tape

Beading thread

Scissors

1 beading needle for each guest

Seed beads (you'll want lots. Get at least one big hank. But you'll probably want several, in different colors.)

An assortment of exotic, interesting beads (look for Moroccan metallic beads, colorful beads with Arabic designs, or whatever strikes your fancy)

1 hook-and-eye clasp for each guest

Clear nail polish

continued on next page

[1] Measure your waist. Cut a piece of beading thread that's 12 inches longer than your waist. Thread it on a beading needle. Then thread on a seed bead, positioning it 6 inches from the end of the thread, so you'll have a 6-inch tail. Take the needle back through the seed bead to make a knot.

[2] String several more seed beads onto the thread. Then add an exotic bead. Continue with the rest of the beads, interspersing exotic beads among the seed beads every few inches or so.

[3] Repeat Step 2 until you've filled the thread, leaving another 6-inch tail.

[4] Take the needle through the last seed bead twice to secure it. Thread a part of the clasp on each end, and knot several times to secure. Snip away the excess thread. Brush the knots with clear nail polish for extra strength.

Kitchen Olympics

If only eating were an Olympic sport. It's the one thing we're really, really good at, and we just know we'd take home the gold.

We're much more interested in frying and fricasseeing than skiing and skating. If you are, too, this slumber party should score high marks. It's a night of food fun and games, and we give it a 10.

This is a pretty casual party that won't require too much prep work. A trip to the grocery store should just about do it. There's no point in decorating, since you're just going to make a mess anyway. Encourage guests to come in clothes they can get a little dirty, and invite an odd number of guests so you will have an even number of participants. You'll provide everyone with a Hot Stuff Apron (page 37) to decorate. Be sure to pick up chef toques for everyone, too.

Movies

Simply Irresistible

Mystic Pizza

Menu

Kitchen Commando Three-Course Dinner*
(If all three courses are inedible,
just order a pizza)

All-night snack offerings: fancy flavored chips, creative gorp, imported cookies

Blender Bender Smoothies* for breakfast

*Recipe follows

Invitation

Write your invitation recipe-style on a pretty recipe card. "Ingredients: 3 cups fun, 2 cups games, 1 ounce music, 4 ounces movies, ¼ teaspoon sleep. Mix everything together at 1724 Paloma Avenue, May 12 at 7:00 p.m."

(Get or make paper ones if you're on a tight budget.) Once everyone's got their game gear on, it's off to the cutting board for a round of Kitchen Commando (page 34). After the kitchen athletes have gotten a good night's rest, head back to the kitchen for a Blender Bender Smoothie competition (page 36). *Bon appétit!*

Music

Duran Duran, "Hungry Like the Wolf"

Weird Al, "Eat It"

Games

We just *know* you won't have a food fight (wink, wink). No, you're *much* too sophisticated for that. But you might enjoy a round of Food Truth or Dare. Dare your friends to eat the craziest food combinations you can think of: ketchup and peanut butter, olives and maple syrup, milk and mustard. Stick to things that are actually edible (no shampoo, please, or the slumber party will end in a doctor's office) and that are intended for humans (Fido won't appreciate you filching his doggie chow). Be warned: If you challenge someone to eat something *too* disgusting, you'll get as good as you gave on the next round. *Yecccch!*

kitchen

commando

Kitchen Commando is a game for gourmet gladiators. It's like a home version of Iron Chef. Split your guests into two teams. Hand each team a bag of surprise ingredients. Then send them off to show what they can do. Let the Grub Games begin!

You will need:

2 sets of 10 surprise ingredients (you can pick anything you like. Here are 10 we recommend: tortillas, shredded cheese, cream cheese, carrots, canned chili, cooked macaroni, saltines, Nutella, whipped topping, and pickles)

2 shopping bags

Microwave Oven

One or more impartial judges

A prize for the winning team

A prize for the losing team (because everyone likes getting prizes; optional)

[1] Load each set of surprise ingredients into a shopping bag. The contents of the shopping bags should be identical. Split your guests into two teams, and give one of the shopping bags to each team.

[2] Each team now has 1 hour to cook a three-course meal, consisting of an appetizer, a main course, and a dessert. They must use every ingredient in the bag, and they may use only the microwave to cook things. Since there's probably only one microwave, each team can use the microwave for only 5 minutes at a time and then must switch off with the other team.

[3] When the hour is up, it's time to eat. Everybody gets to dig in, but only the judges get to assign points. The judges will evaluate the dishes on creativity, taste, and presentation. The team that gets the most points wins a prize. And if you're really nice, you'll give the losers a prize, too.

Note   Keep an adult nearby to supervise. Microwaved food and dishes get hot, and knives are sharp!

blender bender

smoothies

Have you always wondered what peanut butter and peaches would taste like together? Grapefruit and yogurt? Blueberries and lemon juice? Now you can find out. It's make-your-own-smoothie mania.

You will need:

Yogurt

Milk

Juices (orange, apple, pineapple, grapefruit, or whatever you like)

Peanut butter

Honey

Assorted fresh fruits, washed, peeled, and chopped (try berries, melons, bananas, peaches, or whatever you like)

Frozen fruits and berries

Anything else you think would be tasty

Blender

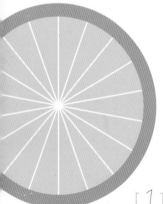

[1] Set out the smoothie fixin's, and give everyone a crack at the blender.

[2] Bottoms up! Be sure to try everyone else's smoothie so you can see which combinations are the tastiest.

hot stuff

aprons

Sure, you're going to get all floury and messy in the kitchen, but that doesn't mean you can't look cute, too. These little aprons are just adorable, and they'll help keep your clothes clean. Whip up a batch for your guests to decorate and take home.

You will need:

Needle and thread

2 lengths of ribbon for each guest, 1 yard each

1 square of fabric for each guest, 18 by 18 inches (cut the edges with pinking shears to prevent fraying)

Fabric paint (puffy paint and glitter paint are especially fun)

Flat-back rhinestones

Fabric glue

[1] You'll want to do this part before the party. Using a needle and thread, secure a 1-yard length of ribbon to a corner of a fabric square with a few stitches. Knot securely. Repeat with another length of ribbon on the other side. Voilà! You now have a cute little apron that ties in the back. Repeat with the rest of the fabric and ribbon until you have enough aprons for all your guests.

continued on next page

[2] Once your guests are assembled, have them decorate their aprons any way they like. They can write their names in fabric paint. Or they can go nuts with the rhinestones and fabric glue.

[3] Let the paint and glue dry. Then put on your aprons and get down, Kitchen Commando style.

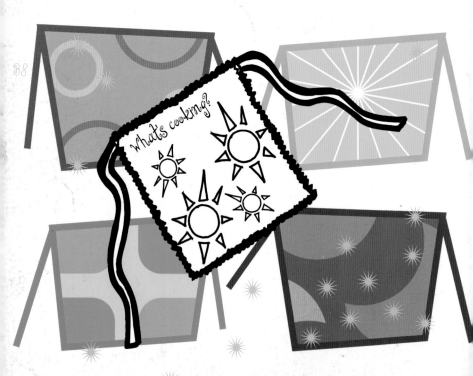

what's cooking?

Fashion Fantasia

Oh, sure, it's not going to change the course of history, but fashion *is* important.

Movies

She's All That

Zoolander

It makes the world a more beautiful place and gives us something to do when there's nothing on TV. Why not plan a party around your favorite pastime? Fashion, darling, fashion!

This party, like your own personal style, can be as simple or as complicated as you want it to be. If you want to go all out, transform the house into a fashion showroom with racks of funky clothes, costumes, and accessories for your guests to try on. Set up a catwalk so they can strut their stuff. Or, if you're into the minimalist

Menu

Fashion plates *(mini flatbread pizzas)*

Tropical print fruit salad

Supermodel Spritzers*

*Recipe follows

Invitation

Use a scanner, a computer, and a color printer to make your invitation look like the cover of a fashion magazine (featuring your beautiful face, of course). If you're technologically impaired, make do with scissors, paste, and a color copier. Be sure to remind your friends to bring a pair of jeans for Jean Genie fun (page 43) and a pile of discarded clothes for the Do-It-Yourself Department Store (page 45).

thing, just buy a stack of fashion magazines to inspire your guests to flights of fashion fancy. Enjoy stylish little snacks like Supermodel Spritzers (page 42), and play Do-It-Yourself Department Store (page 45). Be sure to take lots of pictures of the proceedings. The camera loves you. Work it, baby, work it!

Music

Right Said Fred, "I'm Too Sexy"

Prince, "Raspberry Beret"

RuPaul, "Supermodel (You Better Work)"

Games

There are lots of great fashion games. One of our favorites is Toilet Paper Dress Designer. Divide everyone up into two or more teams. Give each team several rolls of toilet paper. Each team will choose one person as a mannequin and make her a toilet paper "dress" by wrapping her up as stylishly as possible. The cutest dress wins. We also like the game Bundle Up. Start with two teams. Give each team a bag full of clothes. Each team will again choose one person as a mannequin and dress her in all the clothes (without the mannequin's help). The team that dresses its mannequin the fastest wins.

supermodel
spritzers

A girl can work up a thirst stalking the perfect look. This refresher will restore you to cool. It's pretty and sparkly, just like you.

You will need:

6 cups cranberry juice, chilled

6 cups sparkling white grape or apple juice, chilled

4 cups club soda or lemon-lime soda

8 orange slices

8 maraschino cherries

8 drink umbrellas

[1] In a large pitcher, combine the cranberry juice, sparkling grape or apple juice, and soda. Stir.

[2] Pour into 8 large glasses. Garnish each with an orange slice and a cherry speared on a drink umbrella.

Serves 8.

jean genie

Pining for a pair of stylish embellished jeans? Your wish is our command. Transform them with rhinestones, ribbon, patches, and paint. Change dull denim into a designer original.

You will need:

An old pair of jeans for each guest
(or have them bring their own)

Scissors

Decorations: rhinestones, beads, ribbon,
suede fringe, patches, fabric paint, or
whatever you like

Needle and thread or fabric glue

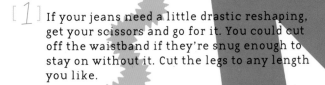

[1] If your jeans need a little drastic reshaping,
get your scissors and go for it. You could cut
off the waistband if they're snug enough to
stay on without it. Cut the legs to any length
you like.

continued on next page

[2] Take your decorations, your needle and thread, or fabric glue and get down. Some ideas:
- Glue rhinestones around the pockets and down the side seams.
- Sew on a sprinkling of beads or a beaded flower.
- Stitch or glue ribbon around the waist or cuffs.
- Adorn the cuffs with suede fringe.
- Sew or glue on patches.
- Paint on hippie-style butterflies, flowers, or hearts.

[3] Allow the paint and glue to dry. Then model your fabulous design.

do-it-yourself
department store

It's 10:00 p.m. and the mall is closed. But the urge to shop is strong. Don't despair! Host a Do-It-Yourself Department Store. Ask guests to bring clothes they love but just can't wear (wrong size, wrong color, whatever). Then swap! Everyone goes home with something new and fabulous.

You will need:

A pile of clothes

[1] There's nothing to it: just set out the goods and let everyone have at it.

[2] If mayhem ensues, assign everyone a number and have them pick one item at a time. The next person can either pick from the pile or poach an item someone else has already picked. The person whose item was poached gets to pick again.

[3] Model your new acquisitions.

Movies

The Princess Diaries

Emma

Pizza and Adam Sandler movies are fine for casual get-togethers, but for special occasions you want something a little more civilized. This party should be just your cup of tea.

Host a proper high tea for proper young ladies. Dress in your finest and speak the Queen's English. Play parlor games and practice your p's and q's. Craft Teatime Tiaras (page 51) and sit for formal Princess Portraits (page 52). Smashing.

Menu

Dainty finger sandwiches
(try cucumber, watercress, herbed cream cheese,
egg salad, or whatever strikes your fancy)

Strawberries and cream

Butter cookies

Pretty Petits Fours*

Hot tea

*Recipe follows

This party will take a bit of planning, but not as much as a royal wedding. All you really need to do is set a beautiful table. Get flowers for the centerpiece and use lace, linen, or a pretty chintz as a tablecloth. Bust out the silver and the good china. If you don't have any, assemble a motley set from a thrift store. Mismatched pieces are fine; they'll lend a funky, shabby-chic touch. Beg or bribe a family member to serve tea in uniform. That will be all, Jeeves.

Games

Put the Sony Playstation away and settle in for a night of classic Victorian parlor games. Maybe you'd enjoy a round of bridge, whist, or cribbage. Or perhaps you'd prefer a rousing game of charades. When everyone starts to get punchy, play Stiff Upper Lip. Have everyone form a circle and instruct them *not* to smile. Designate one person to go into the center. This person's goal is to make the other players laugh. She may make faces, giggle, tease, or do whatever she likes. Whoever laughs becomes "It" and goes into the circle next.

pretty
petits fours

Petits fours are bite-size gateaux with a maximum icing-to-cake ratio. With their pretty pastel glaze, they're almost too pretty to eat. But don't let that stop you.

You will need:

Cake
2 cups flour, sifted

2 teaspoons baking powder

3 eggs

1 cup sugar

½ cup milk

⅓ cup butter, melted

Icing
1 box (16 ounces) powdered sugar

5 tablespoons water

1 teaspoon vanilla extract

Food coloring

Decorations
Candied violets (available at specialty stores), tubes of store-bought decorator frosting, little candies, sprinkles, nuts, or whatever you like

continued on next page

[1] To make the cake, preheat the oven to 350° F. Grease and flour a jelly-roll pan or a 12-by-16-inch baking dish. Combine the flour and baking powder in a medium bowl and set aside.

[2] In a large bowl, use an electric mixer to beat together the eggs and sugar until fluffy and lemon-colored, about 5 minutes. Stir in the milk, then fold in the flour mixture until blended. Add the melted butter and mix well. Spread the batter in the pan and bake for 12 to 15 minutes. Remove from the oven.

[3] Remove the cake from the pan and transfer it to a wire rack. When cool, cut the cake into 1-inch cubes.

[4] To make the icing, in a bowl, combine the powdered sugar, water, and vanilla and mix well. Divide the mixture among 4 bowls and tint it pink, blue, green, and yellow with food coloring. Just use a few drops—you want the icing to be pastel.

[5] To decorate the petits fours, pour the icing over the cake cubes, being sure to coat the tops and sides, and allow to set. Then decorate them as you like.

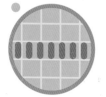

Crafty Girl Shortcut: If you don't have time to make your own cake from scratch, you can use a pound cake mix instead, or simply cut store-bought pound cake into 1-inch cubes.

Serves 8.

teatime

tiaras

Grandmother won't loan you the family jewels? No bother! Craft this easy tiara instead. All you need are some pipe cleaners and glass beads and voilà! You have an instant heirloom.

You will need:

Sparkly cut glass or plastic beads (you'll need 20 to 50 per guest, depending on the size of the beads and how you space them)

Metallic silver pipe cleaners (at least 5 per guest)

[1] Make a base for your tiara by threading some beads on a pipe cleaner. Space them evenly and curve the beaded pipe cleaner in a U shape that will fit on your head.

[2] Thread beads onto the remaining pipe cleaners and add to your tiara by twisting the end of each onto the base and building it up. Make a tiny, tasteful princess-sized tiara or a big Queen Mum–sized one.

[3] Don your tiara and start issuing royal orders.

princess
portraits

Do your friends wear jeans, dirty T-shirts, and baseball caps 24/7? Then you'll want to document the one time they get dressed up. Have everyone sit for formal Princess Portraits. If you have a Polaroid or a digital camera, this makes a great take-home souvenir. If not, send them their portraits after the party. Who knew they could clean up so nice?

You will need:

A nice backdrop (a formal armchair in front of the fireplace is especially nice)

A camera

A pretty frame for each guest

[1] Have each guest sit while you snap their portrait. Instruct them to put on their most ladylike expression. No stuck-out tongues or crossed eyes, please.

[2] If you're using a Polaroid, you're all done. If you're using a digital camera, print the pictures out. If you're using a regular camera, get the pictures developed.

[3] Slip each picture in a pretty frame, and give them to your guests as souvenirs.

Beadapalooza

Are you batty for beads?
Crazy for crystals? Dotty for
Delicas? Does the need to bead
keep you up nights?

Get ready for the best evening of your life. It's an all-night beading session, and you're invited. So bead it!

This is one of the easiest parties to plan. No need to decorate or dress up. Just hit the bead store and load up on supplies. Have some beading books on hand to inspire you and some snacks to sustain you through your beading frenzy. Consider making

Movies

Romancing the Stone

Gentlemen Prefer Blondes
(featuring "Diamonds Are a Girl's Best Friend")

Menu

Veggie wands *(shish kebabs)*

Ruby salad
(tiny toybox tomatoes in vinaigrette)

Jewel Torte*

*Recipe follows

Invitation

Glue beads to a pretty hand-lettered
invitation. If you're really crafty,
include a beaded bracelet or key-
chain as a pre-party souvenir.

yourself a sapphire-colored
choker. It'll match the circles
under your eyes come morning, my beady-eyed friend.

Music

Jewel, of course

Prince, "Diamonds and Pearls"

Games

We suspect you'll be too busy beading to break for games, but if you do, the game of
choice is Treasure Hunt. Before the party, prepare two sets of ten identical clues.
Each clue will lead you to the next one. The first clue might read, "Hear my song.
It goes 'ding dong.' Here I've been, all along." Go to the doorbell and find the next
clue, which will lead you to the washing machine: "Dirty clothes are all she knows. You're
getting close!" The last clue leads to the prize: a treasure chest of beads and beading
supplies. When the guests arrive, divide everyone into two teams. Hand each team the
first clue and send them on their way. The team that gets to the prize first wins it.

jewel torte

This gem of a cake is as pretty as it is tasty. It's made with crushed candies that look like sparkly jewels. You'll wish you could wear it.

You will need:

Cake

1½ cups flour

2 teaspoons baking powder

½ teaspoon salt

½ cup butter

1 cup granulated sugar

2 eggs

1½ teaspoons vanilla extract

½ cup milk

2 rolls fruit-flavored Life Savers, crushed

Icing

6 cups powdered sugar

¾ cup shortening

½ teaspoon salt

1 teaspoon vanilla extract

½ cup plus 2 tablespoons milk

Decoration

2 rolls fruit-flavored Life Savers, crushed

[1] To make the cake, preheat the oven to 350° F. Grease and flour two 8-inch round pans. Combine the flour, baking powder, and salt in a medium bowl and set aside.

[2] In a large bowl, use an electric mixer to cream together the butter and sugar. Add the eggs and vanilla and mix well. Stir in the flour mixture. When the batter is smooth and well blended, mix in the milk and Life Savers. Divide the batter between the pans and bake for 30 minutes, or until a toothpick comes out clean. Remove from the pans and transfer to wire racks to cool.

[3] To make the icing, combine all the icing ingredients in a large bowl and beat with an electric mixer until creamy.

[4] When the cake is cool, frost it with the icing, stacking the layers to make a two-layer cake. Decorate the top and sides with crushed Life Savers.

Crafty Girl Shortcut: Instead of making the cake from scratch, just add crushed Life Savers to a box of white cake mix. Ice with a tub of store-bought white frosting.

Serves 8.

stretchy sparkle
bracelet

How can glamour be so easy? It's crafty beading magic. String sparkly crystals onto elastic cord for an eye-catching stretchy bracelet. The only downside: These bracelets get lonely. Better make a stack of them to wear all at once. Rubies and emeralds and diamonds, oh my!

You will need:

Measuring tape

Elastic beading cord

Scissors

Cut crystal or glass beads (with holes big enough to accommodate the elastic cord)

Clear nail polish

[1] Measure your wrist. Cut a piece of elastic cord a few inches longer.

[2] Thread the cord through the beads.

[3] Knot the ends of the cord securely. Trim the ends and seal with clear nail polish to prevent fraying.

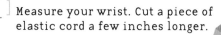

bejeweled
bijoux box

You can't store your beautiful beaded creations in a plain-Jane shoe box. Craft a creation worthy of housing your most precious gems. Your necklaces will think they've moved into a mansion.

You will need:

1 box for each guest (anything will do. Look for cheap wood or papier-mâché boxes at craft stores)

Felt (optional)

Scissors

Good craft glue, such as Aleene's Tacky Glue

Pictures

Clear contact paper

Stickers

Assorted beads

Flat-back jewels

Little toys

Glitter

Sequins

continued on next page

[1] If you want to line your box, cut felt to fit and glue it in place. Allow the glue to set.

[2] If you like, you can affix a few pictures to your box with clear contact paper. Cut pieces of contact paper slightly bigger than each picture. Place the picture face-down on the contact paper, then stick the contact paper to the box. Decorate the box further with your favorite stickers.

[3] Go nuts. Glue on beads, flat-back jewels, little toys, glitter, sequins, or whatever you like. Allow the glue to set.

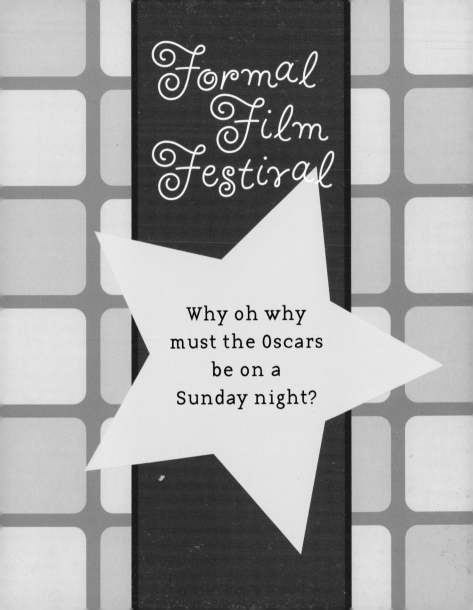

Formal Film Festival

Why oh why must the Oscars be on a Sunday night?

Well, when *you* are nominated, we're sure you'll convince them to move it to Friday or Saturday. In the meantime, celebrate the movies with a party as glamorous as any Hollywood premiere. Roll out the red carpet and greet your gussied-up guests with paparazzi-style flashes and fancy finger food. Then settle in for an evening of high-class cinema. While you watch films or a taped award ceremony, you can make star-styled crafts like Celebrity Sunglasses (page 65) and the Red-Carpet Wrap (page 66).

Movies

Notting Hill

The Big Picture

America's Sweethearts

Menu

Fancy-pants canapés: baked brie, sugared grapes, and Pizza Purses*

Popcorn potpourri: buttered popcorn, cheese popcorn, and caramel popcorn

Dessert buffet: brownies, cookies, or whatever you like

Sparkling apple cider

*Recipe follows

This is definitely a special-occasion party. It will take some planning, but the payoff is a blockbuster slumber party. Start by making a red carpet from red butcher paper. Then decorate the house with movie memorabilia.

Invitation

Make an invitation that looks like a movie poster. "Once Upon a Sleeping Bag. Directed by Julie. Starring Amy, Jessica, Stacy, and Heather. Coming to 848 Camden Way, September 24 at 8:00 p.m."

Ask guests to come in their fanciest gowns, or dressed as celebrities. Sign autographs for each other and catch up on the latest Tinseltown gossip. Munch on fancy flavored popcorn and decadent desserts. Another fabulous party? Of course. You never disappoint your public.

Music

Soundtracks. We especially like *James Bond* music.

Games

There are all kinds of celebrity games. One of our favorites is Celebrity Password. Write the names of twenty or so celebrities on tiny slips of paper, and put them in a bowl. Have guests pair up into two-person teams. One member of a team draws a slip and has to describe the celebrity, without saying the name, until her partner figures out who it is. If she gets it right, the team pulls another name from the bowl and keeps going until 1 minute is up. The team that gets the most right wins.

We also like Celebrity Signs. Write the names of celebrities on pieces of paper and tape them to your guests' backs. Everyone has to figure out whose name they've got on their back from the clues they get from the other guests. So if everyone keeps telling you to hit them, baby, one more time, you'll know you have Britney Spears on your back.

pizza
purses

Pizza gets the red-carpet treatment with these high-class hors d'oeuvres. All your favorite pizza fillings are packed into pretty little pizza purses. They might even match your gown.

You will need:

1 cup pizza sauce

16 puff pastry squares, 5 by 5 inches each, thawed

8 ounces grated mozzarella cheese

1 cup pizza toppings: sliced olives, mushrooms, or whatever you like

[1] Preheat the oven to 400° F. Lightly grease a baking sheet.

[2] Spread a little pizza sauce in the center of each pastry square. Top with cheese and pizza toppings. Pull the corners up into a pouch. Pinch closed and seal the edges with a little water.

[3] Place the pizza purses on the baking sheet and bake for 15 to 18 minutes, or until golden brown. Serve hot.

Makes 16.

celebrity

sunglasses

These snazzy sunglasses will make you look like a star. Even better, they'll shield your peepers from the bright lights of Hollywood. Who's behind those Foster Grants? You are, Crafty Girl.

You will need:

1 pair of sunglasses for each guest (look for cheap ones at a dollar store or a thrift store—the wilder the better)

Good craft glue, such as Aleene's Tacky Glue

Decorations: flat-back rhinestones, pearls, sequins, glitter, feathers, shiny little stickers, or whatever you like

[1] Make sure the glasses are clean and dry. Then glue on your decorations. Don't let good taste hold you back. Go nuts. Let Cher be your muse.

[2] Allow the glue to set. Then slip on your shades and sparkle, darling, sparkle!

red-carpet
Wrap

We'd hate for you to catch a chill while you posed for the paparazzi. This sheer, diaphanous wrap will keep your shoulders warm without covering up your gown. Decorate with boa trim, sequins, or glitter for extra glamour. Fabulous!

You will need:

1 piece of fabric for each guest, 18 by 60 inches (sheer fabrics like organza are especially nice)

Sewing machine or pinking shears

1 smock for each guest (so they won't get glue on their gowns)

Decorations: glitter fabric paint, beads, sequins, flat-back rhinestones, boa trim, or whatever you like

Fabric glue

1   You'll want to do this part before your guests arrive. Using a sewing machine, turn the edges of each piece of fabric under 1/4 inch or so and sew them down to prevent fraying. Or, if you're allergic to sewing, simply trim the edges with pinking shears.

2   Once your guests are assembled, set out the smocks, decorations, and fabric glue and let them go at it. They can paint on butterflies or stars or glue on sequins or beads or boa trim. Let the glue set. Then hit the red carpet.

Esmerelda de Levant, a wealthy,
eccentric recluse, has died under
mysterious circumstances. She's left
her entire fortune to you. There's only
one catch: You have to spend the night
in her quite-possibly-haunted house.
Who knows what terrors await you?

Night on
Haunted Hill

This party is great for Halloween or Friday the 13th. It may take a lot of planning, but when you see your friends' horror-stricken faces it will all be worth it. Transform your house into a decrepit manor. Start outside by placing Esmerelda's headstone in the front yard (and if you have a prop hand, make sure it's crawling out of the ground). Drape spider webs all over. Get some dry ice for an extra-spooky foggy atmosphere. Leave the lights off in front, and tape an ominous sign to the front door: "Come in. We're expecting you."

Inside, more signs direct guests to a room well inside the house, where each one is greeted by hair-raising screams from the guests who've already arrived. Then let the games begin. Have a dark and dreary dinner, make creepy crafts, watch scary movies, and play terrifying games. Ask a family member to dress as Esmerelda and silently pass by the room at odd intervals. Make sure you've got plenty of spooky sound effects.

Movies

The Addams Family

The Sixth Sense

Menu

Ghoulash*

Vampire bane *(garlic bread)*

Cemetery field greens *(salad)*

Scum cake
(frost a chocolate cake with slimy green frosting)

*Recipe follows

Invitation

On a parchment scroll, write "Esmerelda de Levant has passed away under extremely mysterious circumstances and has named you as heir to her substantial fortune. But in order to claim your inheritance, you must spend the night in her haunted mansion. Come, if you dare, October 31 at 8:00 p.m."

Have the lights flicker a lot and, at some point, go out entirely.

Sleep if you dare.

Note: You can get dry ice at party-supply stores and some ice cream shops. Be warned: It will cause severe burns if you touch it, so wear gloves and handle it carefully. Better yet, leave it to a grown-up. And if your friends, siblings, or pets can't be trusted to stay away from it, skip it entirely.

Music

Spooky sound effects
Bobby "Boris" Pickett, "Monster Mash"

Games

So many good scary games, so little time. You'll definitely want to play the classics. Start with Bloody Mary. Stand before a mirror and see if you're brave enough to chant "Bloody Mary" three times. Who knows what terror you might invoke! Then move on to Light as a Feather, Stiff as a Board. One guest must lie on the floor while everyone else forms a circle around her, placing two fingers of each hand under her body. Chant "Light as feather, stiff as a board" and try to lift her. Will she levitate? And don't forget And Then There Was One. Also known as Sardines, this game is the opposite of Hide and Go Seek. The person who is "It" hides, and everyone else tries to find her. When they do, they hide with her. Eventually, only one person is left, looking for all the others. This person is "It" for the next round. Finally, if you have time, play Esmerelda's Remains. Prepare a bowl with two peeled grapes, a bowl of cooked spaghetti, and a bowl of cold cooked oatmeal. Lead your guests into a completely dark room and then, one by one, place their hands in each bowl, solemnly intoning, "These are Esmerelda's eyes. These are Esmerelda's guts. These are Esmerelda's brains." Ick!

ghoulash

It may sound gross, but this dish is actually ghoulishly good. Pasta, sauce, ricotta, and mozzarella cheese combine for a soupy, goopy, yummy dinner. Eye of newt is optional.

You will need:

2 jars (26 to 28 ounces each) pasta sauce

4 cups water

6 cups uncooked pasta (use rotelle, bowties, or whatever you like)

2 tubs (15 ounces each) ricotta cheese

4 cups shredded mozzarella cheese

[1] In a large saucepan, combine the pasta sauce, water, and pasta over medium-high heat. Bring to a boil. Reduce the heat to low. Cover and cook for 15 minutes.

[2] Add the ricotta cheese. Cover and cook for 5 more minutes. Remove from the heat. Stir in half the mozzarella cheese, and sprinkle the rest on top. Cover and let stand for 5 minutes, or until the cheese is melted. Serve in bowls.

Serves 8.

sorceress
slime

Bust out the cauldron and chemicals, witchie-poo; it's time to make a potion. It won't make anyone fall in love with you, it won't make you rich, and it won't let you the see the future. But it will produce a truly disgusting slime that's loads of fun to play with, and that's sort of magical, isn't it?

You will need:

2 teaspoons psyllium husks or psyllium-based laxative like Metamucil

2½ cups water

A few drops food coloring

[1] Combine all the ingredients in a large ceramic or glass bowl and place in the microwave. Microwave for 6 minutes, or until the mixture is just about to bubble over. Turn the microwave off, but don't remove the bowl. Wait a minute or so, then repeat the cooking process several times, until the mixture looks good and slimy.

continued on next page

[2] Using a potholder, remove the bowl from the microwave. *Don't touch the slime.* It is hot hot hot. We mean it. Let it cool for at least an hour before handling. In the meantime, you can give it a couple stirs with a spoon.

[3] When the slime is cold and clammy, dig in. If you plan on having a slime fight, be warned: it will stain whatever it lands on. So wear aprons and stay away from the white upholstery. We doubt you'd want to put something this gross in your mouth, but we'll caution you anyway: It's not edible.

poison ring

Poison rings are pretty jeweled rings with something extra: a secret compartment. They used to be used for storing herbs or potions, but you can use yours to store lip gloss.

You will need:

1 paintbrush for each guest

1 teeny-tiny empty metal container with lid (such as an old lip gloss container) for each guest

Gold or silver paint

Flat-back gems

Good craft glue, such as Aleene's Tacky Glue

1 ring blank (available at craft and bead stores) for each guest

Epoxy

[1] Using a paintbrush, paint the metal container with gold or silver paint. You may need several coats. Allow the paint to dry completely after each coat.

continued on next page

[2] When the paint is dry, glue flat-back gems on the container, using good craft glue.

[3] Glue the metal container to a ring blank with epoxy. Allow to set before wearing the ring.

Slumber Party in the Beauty Salon

Ever wished you could spend
the night at Chez Beauté?
Tonight's your chance.

Get ready, girls, for all-out, all-night goof-ball glamour treatments. Give each other manic makeovers, wild up-dos, and over-the-top manicures. Dahhhling, you look vonnnnderful!

76

This party will take a bit of planning, but beauty is worth the effort. Transform your house into an old-school beauty salon. Drape the furniture with pink sheets. If you can get a barber's chair or an old-fashioned cone hair-dryer, you are the coolest host of all time. If not, establish the salon atmosphere by hanging up some mirrors and setting out a display of shampoo, hairbrushes, and hot rollers. Make sure the coffee table is

Movies

Hairspray

Funny Face

Miss Congeniality

Menu

Avocado mousse

Wacky snackies
(make campy canapés from your favorite sixties cookbook, or just serve store-bought frozen tidbits)

Powder Puffs*

*Recipe follows

Invitation

Tape your invitation to travel-sized bottles of shampoo, making it look as much like the shampoo label as possible. Lather, rinse, repeat!

loaded with beauty magazines. Tear out a few of your favorite pictures to frame and hang. Set up a Beauty Bar and stock it with makeup, nail polish, and hair products of all kinds. Load up on the wild stuff: spray-on hair color, green nail polish, turquoise eye shadow, and magenta mascara. Encourage guests to help themselves. Get some old-fashioned salon smocks to protect your guests' outfits. And have plenty of cold cream on hand, or your night of beauty could turn into an ugly morning.

Music

Hair bands, of course:

Bon Jovi, Poison, Heart, B-52's, Go-Go's

Games

It's our favorite slumber party game of all time: Mystery Makeover. One by one, send each guest into a mirrorless room with a lipstick, blush, eye shadow, and eyebrow pencil. She has 1 minute to apply all the makeup by herself without a mirror. Whoever looks the most ridiculous wins.

powder puffs

These little puffs are for your mouth, not your nose.
They're filled with whipped cream and dusted with
powdered sugar. Beautiful.

You will need:

Pastries
1½ cups water

¾ cup butter

1½ cups flour, sifted

6 eggs, at room temperature

Filling
2 cups whipping cream

1 teaspoon vanilla extract

¼ cup powdered sugar

Topping
¼ cup powdered sugar

[1] To make the pastries, preheat the oven to
375° F. Grease 2 baking sheets.

[2] In a large saucepan, combine the water and butter over high heat and bring to a boil. Lower the heat to medium and add the flour all at once, mixing well. When the mixture pulls away from the sides of the pan, remove from the heat and allow to cool for 5 minutes. Then stir in the eggs, one at a time, mixing vigorously.

[3] Plop generous spoonfuls of batter onto baking sheets, spacing them 2 inches apart. Bake for 30 minutes, or until the pastries are golden. Remove from the oven and transfer to wire racks. When cool, slice the tops off and scoop out the insides.

[4] To make the filling, use an electric mixer to whip the cream with the vanilla and sugar in a large bowl until stiff peaks form. Remove the tops of the pastries and fill with the whipped cream mixture. Replace the tops and sift powdered sugar over them.

[5] Chill until ready to serve.

Makes 16 large puffs.

makeover

mania

Want a little vacation from your usual self? Stock up on makeup, wild accessories, and wigs. Have your friends bring their own makeup, too. Then take turns giving each other radical makeovers. Transform your preppy best friend into a punk rock princess or your tomboy friend into a demure darling. Be sure to photograph each new look. Give your friends copies, or hang on to them for future blackmailing. Clean up with lots of cotton balls and cold cream!

You will need:

A camera

Crazy costumes and accessories

Wigs and partial wigs, like ponytails, braids, and buns you can pin on

Hair products: mousse, hair spray, gel, spray-on temporary hair color

Hair appliances: hot rollers, curling iron, crimping iron

Gobs of makeup in crazy colors

[1] Take a "before" picture of each victim.

[2] Go nuts. Dress them up in wild outfits. Add wigs or style their own hair in a crazy 'do. Give them a bouffant, spikes, or Pippi-style braids. Then spackle on a load of makeup. Say Cheese!

pucker up pink-lemonade
lip gloss

When life gives you lemons, make lip gloss. This fun and fruity lip gloss mixes up in minutes. How refreshing!

You will need:

1 cup solid shortening

½ cup powdered pink lemonade

8 clean, dry containers (use old lip gloss containers or 35-mm film canisters)

[1] Cream together the shortening and lemonade mix in a glass measuring cup until well mixed.

[2] Microwave on high for 2 to 3 minutes, or until melted.

[3] Pour the mixture into the containers and allow to cool completely.

Rock Star Karaoke Corral

If you want to rock and roll all night and party every day, this is the slumber party for you. Live the rock star life for twelve hours. Sing your heart out, scarf endless junk food, and party with your posse. Rock on!

83

Movies

Josie and the Pussycats
Spice World

Menu

Elvis Sandwiches*

Tutti frutti fruit salad

Backstage junk food buffet
(chips, cookies, whatever you like)

*Recipe follows

This party takes almost no preparation. All you'll need is a karaoke machine and some CDs. Most DVD players and some stereos have a karaoke feature. If yours doesn't, you can easily rent a karaoke machine. You can get karaoke CDs at any record store. Tell

Invitation

Buy a bunch of CD cases and insert the invitation like a CD cover. If you're pulling out all the stops, you could even burn a custom CD to include as a pre-party souvenir.

your guests to come dressed as their favorite rock stars, and stock up on temporary tattoos to help them get into the rock-and-roll spirit. String up some flashing lights and you're all set. Now all you need to do is practice your power ballad. Your audience will definitely demand an encore.

Music

Anything goes

Games

You could play a home version of *Name That Tune*—play a couple bars of a song and see who can guess it in the fewest notes. Or play a songwriting game. Break everyone up into pairs and assign them all different topics and musical genres. You could, for instance, ask them to write a country song about the time you all went to the water-slide park, or a blues song about the time you all got detention. Then have everyone perform. The best song wins a standing ovation and a prize.

elvis

sandwiches

The king of rock and roll knew a thing or two about eating. Rich, salty, and sweet all at once, this may be the most delicious sandwich in the history of the world. It's like a hunk of burning love.

You will need:

16 slices white bread

8 bananas, mashed

1 cup peanut butter

About ½ cup margarine

[1] Make 8 sandwiches on white bread, spreading a banana and 2 tablespoons of peanut butter on each.

[2] Melt 2 tablespoons of the margarine in a large frying pan over medium-high heat. Then fry the sandwiches, 2 or 3 at a time, adding more margarine as necessary. Cook until golden brown on both sides.

Makes 8 sandwiches.

rhinestone
rocker tee

That concert tee was the coolest thing in the world the day after the show. Now it's a little blah. Rescue it with some rhinestones. A little glue, a little glitter, and it's rock-star ready again.

You will need:

1 concert T-shirt for each guest (anything will do, from boy bands to retro rockers. Get funny retro ones on the cheap at a thrift store. Look for hair bands, metal monsters, disco divas, and one-hit wonders. If you find a Flock of Seagulls shirt, you're our hero.)

Washable fabric glue

Flat-back rhinestones

Scissors (optional)

1 Put on some rockin' music to get yourself in the right mood. Then get your T-shirt, your glue, and your rhinestones, and go nuts. Glue rhinestones wherever you want. Give Madonna a rhinestone beauty mark and sparkly hair. Glitter up Billy Idol's sneer or Britney's belly button. Glue a sprinkling of rhinestones in the background. Allow the glue to set.

2 If your tee still isn't as retro or rockin' as you like, indulge in a little judicious cutting. Cut off the collar, the sleeves, or the hem. Add some punk rock slashes and safety pins. Then put on your tee, crank the music to 11, and rock out, Crafty Girl style.

ROCK STAR

video~la~la

Want a souvenir that will remind you how much fun your party was? That will embarrass you for years to come? Then you need to make your own video. Put on your favorite CD, get dressed in crazy costumes, and lip-synch for the camera. If you're really nice, you'll dub copies for all your friends. And if your friends are really nice, they won't show it to everyone at school.

You will need:

Costumes

Your favorite CD

Video camera

[1] Put out your craziest costumes and let everyone pick an outfit.

[2] Once everyone's dressed, fire up the CD, flip on the video camera, and film what happens.

Bliss-Out Spa Party

Quizzes, crushes,
complexion crises
. . . life can be
so stressful.

If you and your friends are feeling burned out, it's time to host a spa party. Invite everyone over for a night of beauty treatments and spa food. Then sleep like pampered, exfoliated, well-moisturized babies.

90

Movies

Bring It On

Romy and Michelle's High School Reunion

Menu

Movie Star Salad*

Make-your-own-sundae bar *(what is more calming than hot fudge?)*

*Recipe follows

This is a great party for the last day of finals. No need to stress yourself out—the prep is minimal. Just have some basic beauty supplies, escapist movies, and indulgent snacks on hand. Light

Invitation

Write the invitation up in your prettiest, most flowery handwriting, and include an envelope of bath salts.

some candles and play soothing music. Tell your guests to bring bathrobes and slippers and make themselves comfortable. Give each other massages, manicures, pedicures, and facials. And give your skin and hair some first aid with the Overnight Repair Kit (page 95). The next morning you'll be ready to take on the world again. Or if not the world, at least high school.

Music

Enya or rainforest sounds

Games

If you're up for a little diversion, play a round of What's That Scent. Find six different fragrant beauty products (shampoo, scented lotion, cologne, etc.) and hide them in a bag. Give everyone a piece of paper and a pen and blindfold them. Wave each product under their noses, and have them write down what they think the product is. (They can remove their blindfolds while they write, but be sure you keep the products out of view.) Whoever gets the most right wins.

movie star
salad

This salad makes a light, delicious spa dinner. The infusion of vitamins is sure to restore you to your energetic self. The best part: It will leave plenty of room for dessert.

You will need:

Dressing

¾ cup mayonnaise

1 teaspoon Dijon mustard

1 clove garlic, minced

½ teaspoon ground black pepper

½ teaspoon sugar

1 tablespoon finely chopped celery

Salad

2 heads lettuce, washed and torn into small pieces

4 tomatoes, chopped

6 hard-boiled eggs

2 avocados, chopped

1½ cups crumbled or cubed cheese (blue cheese is best, but if that's too strong for you, pick Swiss or something milder)

2 cups sweet corn kernels

1 cup chopped celery

1 cup chopped green onions

1 cup cashews (optional)

[1] To make the dressing, combine the dressing ingredients in a measuring cup and mix well. Cover and refrigerate.

[2] To make the salad, combine all the salad ingredients except the cashews in a large bowl. Pour the dressing over the top and toss well. Toss in the cashews, if desired, and serve immediately.

Serves 8.

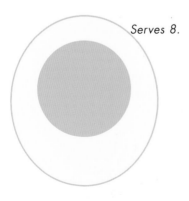

lavender luxe

eye pillow

Oh, what your eyes have seen: really bad movies, four hours of homework a night, zit breakouts. No wonder they're tired. Make them this little pillow and give them a rest.

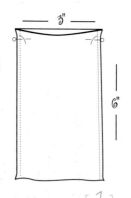

You will need:

1⅓ cups flax seed for each guest

2 tablespoons dried lavender for each guest

1 piece of fabric for each guest, 12 by 3 inches (pick something that will feel nice, like velvet or satin)

Straight pins

Needle and thread

[1] Mix the flax seed and lavender together in a large measuring cup and set aside.

[2] Fold the fabric strip in half so the right sides are facing. Pin in place. Sew the side seams as shown. Turn right-side out.

[3] Fill the sleeve with the flax seed mixture. Tuck the raw edges under at the top, and sew the pillow shut.

repair kit

Are your ends split? Are your hands soft as sandpaper? Do your heels look like hooves? Baby, you need some help. These overnight beauty treatments will set you right. Just slather them on and get some beauty rest. That's better.

Hands and Feet

You will need:

¼ cup solid shortening

½ cup almond or olive oil

1 tablespoon cocoa butter

1 pair cotton gloves for each guest
(available at drugstores)

1 pair cotton socks for each guest

[1] Combine the shortening, oil, and cocoa butter in a saucepan over low heat until melted. Remove from the heat.

[2] Let the mixture cool a little, then whip with an electric mixer until a creamy lotion forms.

[3] When the mixture is still slightly warm, slather the lotion on your hands and feet. Slip on gloves and socks and hit the sack.

continued on next page

Hair

You will need:

1½ tablespoons olive oil for each head

4 drops essential oil for each head (optional; use chamomile for blonde hair, rosemary for red or dark hair)

1 old towel for each head

[1] Mix the olive oil and essential oil, if desired, together and work through your dry hair from roots to ends.

[2] Place an old towel over your pillow so you won't get it all greasy.

[3] In the morning, shampoo the oil out.

The Crystal Ball

Looooook
into the crystal
ball. What do you see?
There is mist . . . and
mystery . . . and laughter.
Eight girls are smiling. . .
They are sitting on velvet
pillows, eating exotic pastries, drinking tea, and
examining each
other's palms.

We see the future, and it's a night of fortune-telling fun and gypsy flavor.

This party will take some planning, but a gifted gypsy like yourself is up to the challenge. Dress the part by tying a fortune-teller-style scarf on your head and wearing lots of jangly jewelry. Transform the house into a proper gypsy camp with peasant-patterned scarves, woven rugs, embroidered pillows, and cozy quilts. Set the mood with some mysterious mist, courtesy of dry ice. Ward off the evil eye with folky plaques and amulets. Dinner is an indoor picnic served on a low table. For a centerpiece, make a crystal ball by freezing a small water balloon and cutting away the balloon once the water

Movies

Love Potion #9
Practical Magic

Menu

Bohemian Bites*

Wild salad of field greens

Chocolate rhapsody
(dark chocolate brownie wedges)

*Recipe Follows

Invitation

Make an invitation that looks like a tarot card, decorated with woodcut-style illustrations.

is frozen. Then make some tea and see what the leaves have to say. Is there love or luck in your future? We can't say, but a fabulous slumber party seems like a sure bet.

Note: You can get dry ice at party-supply stores and some ice cream shops. Be warned: It will cause severe burns if you touch it, so wear gloves and handle it carefully. Better yet, leave it to a grown-up. And if your friends, siblings, or pets can't be trusted to stay away from it, skip it entirely.

Music

Cher, "Gypsies, Tramps, and Thieves"

Balkan choral music

Games

Feeling lucky? Then play a round of Fortune's Wheel. Make a wheel out of cardboard or a paper plate. Attach a dial using a brad. Divide the wheel into eight colors that correspond to eight colored envelopes. Inside each envelope, place a different party favor: a gift certificate for an ice cream cone, sparkly barrettes, or whatever little things you think your friends might like. Each guest takes a spin. Whoever lands on red gets the red envelope, whoever lands on yellow gets the yellow envelope, and so on. If someone lands on a color that's already been taken, she spins again.

bohemian
bites

Also known as Beggars' Purses, these little treats are traditionally made with crêpes, but we've taken a shortcut here and used tortillas. These purses are too small for a wallet or a lipstick, but they're stuffed to bursting with a delicious spinach and cheese filling. An accessory has never been so tasty.

You will need:

2 tablespoons butter

2 tablespoons chopped onion

1 package (10 ounces) frozen chopped spinach, thawed

1 cup ricotta cheese

1 cup shredded Monterey Jack cheese

¼ cup crumbled feta cheese

Salt and pepper to taste

16 flour tortillas, 8 inches in diameter

Cooking twine

Oil for frying

[1] Melt the butter in a sauté pan. Add the onion and spinach and sauté until the onion is translucent.

[2] Transfer the spinach mixture to a large bowl. Add the ricotta, Monterey Jack, feta, and salt and pepper. Mix well.

[3] If the tortillas are stiff, warm them up a bit in the microwave, then place 2 heaping tablespoons of filling in the center of each tortilla. Gather the edges and tie with twine, so the tortilla resembles a purse.

[4] Have an adult do this part. Hot oil can be very dangerous. Heat 1 inch of oil in a frying pan. Fry the purses for 1 or 2 minutes, or until golden brown. Drain on paper towels. Remove the twine (be careful not to burn your fingers!) and serve.

Makes 16.

queen of the gypsies
skirt

A gypsy needs a skirt with flair. This fanciful flounced skirt has got that and then some. Bedecked and beribboned, it's utterly beguiling. Now work that skirt!

You will need:

1 secondhand skirt for each guest (or have them bring their own; ruffled skirts are best)

Fabric glue

Needle and thread

An assortment of pretty ribbon

Rick-rack trim in several colors

Coin charms or bells

[1] Get your skirt and go for it. Glue or stitch on ribbon and rick-rack trim. Don't hold back. Really stripe that skirt up.

[2] Make a fringe by stitching some coin charms or bells to the hem. Now when you dance, you'll provide some music, too!

fortune-telling
411

Need the 411 on fortune-telling? Here's the lowdown on two classic methods. Try them both. Whichever method predicts a life of perfect unending happiness is the one you should swear by.

Tea Leaves

Next to fortune cookies, this is the tastiest way to learn what your future holds.

You will need:

1 cup water for each guest

1 tablespoon loose tea leaves for each guest

[1] Bring the water to a boil, pour into a teacup, and add the tea leaves. Allow to steep for 5 minutes.

[2] Drink up and mellow out. When there are only a few sips of tea left, think of a question. Swirl the tea around, then look in your cup. What you see in the leaves is your answer. Is that happily-ever-after you see? Yes, I think so.

continued on next page

Palmistry

Palmistry, or chiromancy, is one of the oldest methods of fortune-telling. What does your hand foretell?

You will need:

Clean hands

[1] Using the chart, examine the important lines of the hand. Are they long and continuous, without irregularities? Which lines are strongest? These are the parts of your life that are going best.

[2] Next, consider the color of each line. Pink indicates health and optimism; yellow, bitterness; deep red, anger; and blue, loneliness. So, if your life line is pink, lucky you!

[3] Finally, consider the nail polish. This is not tradition- ally part of the palmistry process, but we think your choice of polish says a lot about you. Do you have a demure French manicure? This means you're going to marry Monsieur Tranquil. And if your nails are spangly blue, you're going to be a famous rock star.

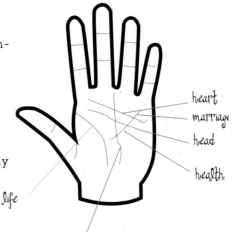

heart
marriage
head
health
life
fate

Think Pink

Sometimes the best
parties have the simplest
themes—say,
just a color or two.

The most famous party of all time was Truman Capote's Black and White Ball. And the most fun we ever had was at a Purple and Orange Party. If simple is your style, we've got two words for you: Think Pink. Host a pink party and we're sure it'll come up roses.

Movies

Pretty in Pink

Pink Panther

Legally Blonde

Menu

Pink patties
(croquettes made from chicken, cheese, or whatever you like, tinted with red food coloring)

Pink potatoes
(mashed potatoes tinted with red food coloring)

Pink cupcakes

Pink Parfaits*

Pink drinks
(our favorite: milk with grenadine in a tall glass with a cherry garnish)

*Recipe follows

Your pink party can be as plain or fancy as you want it to be. Start by swathing the house in pink. Use sheets, streamers, balloons, and flowers. Pink is more than a color; it's an attitude and an aesthetic. Indulge in pink activities, like styling

Invitation

Hot pink pen on pale pink paper, of course

each other's hair and dishing the dirt. Serve pink food and pink drinks. Watch pink-themed movies and play pink-themed music. Be sure to instruct guests to wear you-know-what. Frankly, you're doing them a favor. *Everyone* looks good in pink.

Music

Nick Drake, "Pink Moon"
Edith Piaf, "La Vie en Rose"

Games

You simply *must* play a round of Tickled Pink. Also known as the Ha Ha Game, it's simple and silly and it'll have you in stitches. Have everyone lie on the floor. Everyone should have her head on someone else's stomach. The first person to go says "Ha." The second person says "Ha Ha," the third person says "Ha Ha Ha," and so on. The object is to go as long as you can without laughing. We doubt you'll get as far as "Ha Ha Ha Ha."

pink parfaits

Aren't all the best foods pink? Lemonade, bubble gum, cotton candy, peppermint ice cream . . . they just wouldn't be the same if they were green. Here's another dish to add to your list of great pink desserts. Layers of raspberry mousse, raspberry sauce, and whipped cream make a parfait that's pink perfection.

You will need:

4 cups fresh or frozen raspberries, washed or thawed

½ cup granulated sugar

3 cups whipping cream

½ cup powdered sugar

8 parfait glasses

[1] Combine the raspberries and granulated sugar in a blender or food processor and process until you have a well-blended sauce. Set aside.

[2] Using an electric mixer, whip the cream with the powdered sugar until stiff peaks form. Set a third of the whipped cream aside in a separate bowl.

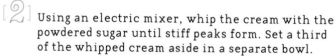

[3] Fold all but 1 cup of the raspberry sauce into the larger bowl of whipped cream. Gently mix well until you have a nice, fluffy raspberry mousse.

[4] In the parfait glasses, layer the raspberry mousse, the remaining raspberry sauce, and the plain whipped cream.

Serves 8.

rosette

manicure

*Pink lipstick, pink blush, pink eye shadow . . . what's missing?
Oh, of course! Paint your paws with pretty pink flowers.*

You will need:

Pale pink nail polish

Dark pink nail polish

Green nail polish

Clear topcoat

[1] Start by brushing on a couple of coats
of pale pink polish. Allow to dry.

[2] Using dark pink polish, dot a 5-petaled flower
on each nail. Add a green stem. Allow to dry.

[3] Finish up with a protective clear topcoat.

ring around
the rosy

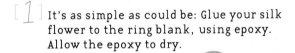

Complement your Rosette Manicure with an easy, pink flower ring. Wear it on your pinkie, of course. Or, make one for each finger and you'll have a portable flower garden.

You will need:

1 little pink silk flower (flat flowers like gerbera daisies work best) for each guest

1 ring blank (available at craft and bead stores) for each guest

Epoxy

[1] It's as simple as could be: Glue your silk flower to the ring blank, using epoxy. Allow the epoxy to dry.

Want to throw a party that's as big as all outdoors? Host an alfresco fiesta! Invite the whole troop over and camp out in the backyard.

This is a great way to celebrate the end of school and the start of summer. Take the theme in any direction you like. You could go with a scouting motif and assign quirky awards like the Junk Food Badge (for eating the most potato chips) or the Bling Bling Badge (for the most stylish uniform). You could have a summer camp motif

Movies

Movies in the wilderness? What, are you kidding me? But if you must, we suggest:

Castaway

Meatballs

Menu

Castaway cookout
(fire up the barbee and grill whatever you like)

Potato salad

Grilled corn on the cob

Watermelon

Backyard Brownie Dirt Bowls*

Recipe follows

Invitation

Go rustic. Make your invitation look like a tattered wilderness guide or treasure map. You could even roll it up and put it in a bottle.

and serve completely inedible food. Or you could go with a castaway/Gilligan's Island theme and sleep in the sand. Try to make a skateboard out of coconuts and palm fronds!

Whichever theme you choose, we're sure you'll have a blast. It's survival of the funnest!

Music

Tropical tunes or campfire songs

Games

Plan a bunch of reward challenges for your intrepid guests. You could set up a backyard obstacle course, host a treasure hunt, or have a tent-decorating competition.

backyard brownie
dirt bowls

Dirt, sludge, and worms? Yes, please! This disgusting dessert looks like compost and tastes like candy. Who knew mulch could be so yummy?

You will need:

1 box brownie mix

4 cups cold milk

2 packages instant chocolate pudding

1 tub whipped topping, thawed

8 plastic cups

Gummy worms

[1] Make the brownies according to the package directions. Cool and cut into 24 squares.

[2] Leave 16 brownie squares out, uncovered, to get a little stale. Once they've gotten a little dry, put them in a resealable plastic bag and smash them into crumbs.

continued on next page

[3] In a large bowl, combine the milk and pudding mix. Whisk until well mixed. Let stand for 5 minutes, then fold in the whipped topping and half the brownie crumbs you made in step 2.

[4] Place a brownie in the bottom of each plastic cup. Fill the cups with pudding mixture. Top with the rest of the brownie crumbs and the gummy worms. Make sure some worms hang over the edge—it looks extra-gross. Serve immediately, before the worms wriggle away.

Serves 8.

castaway

clothes

We love camping out, but cargo shorts and hiking boots don't quite do it for us. We prefer this hot halter and sarong set. It's not exactly practical for rock climbing, but it's perfect for poolside.

You will need:

2¼ yards lightweight fabric for each guest

Pinking shears

Needle and thread

3 yards silk cord for each guest

[1] First, make your sarong. Cut a 1 ¾-yard length of fabric. Go around all the edges with pinking shears, to prevent fraying. That's it! Wrap your sarong around your waist and secure it by tying the top 2 corners in a knot.

continued on next page

[2] To make the halter, cut a 20-by-20-inch square of fabric. Trim the edges with pinking shears to prevent fraying. Fold in half to form a triangle. Using your needle and thread, stitch a seam 1 inch from the bottom as shown. Then fold the top of the triangle down about 2 inches. Pin in place. Sew a seam 1 inch from the top as shown. If the two layers of the halter are really flopping loose of one another, tack sides together with a few stitches.

[3] Cut a 2-yard length of silk cord and thread it through the tube you made at the bottom of the halter. Thread the remaining 1-yard length of silk cord through the tube at the top. Then tie on your halter and go recline on a chaise longue.

1"

1"

audio

scavenger hunt

Sure, scavenger hunts are fun, but you end up with slightly annoyed neighbors and twenty pieces of junk you don't really want. Orphaned socks, dead batteries, and soy sauce packets? No thanks. Host an audio scavenger hunt instead. It's even more fun than the old way, and you won't generate any more landfill.

You will need:

A list of 15 or so sounds (make 2 copies)

2 tape recorders

2 blank tapes

[1] Before the party, write up the list of 15 or so sounds for players to track down. Some ideas: a car horn, a dog bark, running water, a bird call, middle C on a piano, 10 seconds of a sitcom theme song, a soda can opening, a baby talking or crying, 10 seconds of the news, a lawnmower, a motorcycle, a balloon popping, crickets, a bat hitting a ball, the ice cream truck.

[2] At the party, divide everyone up into 2 teams. Give each team a copy of the list, a tape recorder, and a blank tape and send them on their way. The team that tapes all 15 sounds and makes it back to the house first wins.